Living on the Borderline

Lauren Philpott

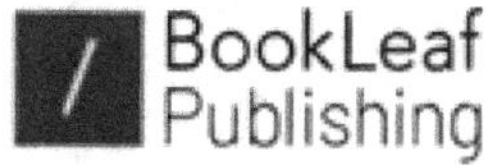

Presentation by *BookLeaf Publishing*

Web: www.bookleafpub.com

E-mail: info@bookleafpub.com

ISBN: 9789357213042

First edition 2023

Waves

I have never been so scared
of my own head

Of what I tell myself. What I make myself
believe.
Is it true? Is it lies? Will I ever know?
The thoughts, they come and go, like waves.

Except...

Waves are relaxing. Waves wash over you
calmly.
These thoughts are a storm.
They crash. They're consuming. They're quickly
overwhelming.

Yeah, they retreat, but only to gather momentum
so they can crash back harder.

And trying to stay afloat?
Well, that's exhausting.

The Vicious Cycle

There's a stigma with this illness that we are liars
and sneaks.
We're all manipulative and are just trying to play
you.

Maybe the reason for this is because
you don't trust or believe us,
or even try to understand.

So if you don't believe what we tell you,
we'll tell you what you want to hear.

At least that gets you off our backs.

The Decision

3

Will it be the end of the world if you eat that?

Will it be the end of the world if I don't?

The Words We Use

Think about the words we use
when going about our day
do they have negative connotations?
What do we really say?

When something happens that surprises us,
or we think someone's strange
words like 'Mad'; Insane'; 'Nuts'; 'Crackers';
'that person is deranged!'

'Crazy'; 'Barmy'; 'Bonkers'; 'Psycho';
it's like an unstoppable flow
But what is this saying about mental health?
The stigma continues to grow.

So what can we say instead of these words
to improve the message we send?
Words such as 'Remarkable'; 'Extraordinary';
Astonishing';
Are much less likely to offend.

There are others too; the list can go on:
'Phenomenal'; 'Incredible'; 'Unexpected';
'Marvellous'; 'Wonderful'; 'Unfounded'; 'Bizarre'.
We will no longer be disrespected.

The Fog

The fog is getting thicker
The waves are getting higher.
I can see the way out but I won't take it.
There's no block, no obstacle;
except my head.

I won't let myself.
Fear is in the way
and I'm not brave enough
to take the plunge.

If I Eat

If I eat, how will anyone know
how much I'm hurting?

They think if I eat, I'm fine.

My Friend Ana

Anorexia?

Huh.

She's a tricky bitch.

Just when you think you've got her all worked
out,
she gets you another way.

There's no way out.
My friend Ana has me wrapped around her
finger.

You Don't Know What It's Like

You don't know what it's like to feel hollow, empty. To not even have a vague sense of who you are, or what you want.

You don't know what it's like to have that shadow following you around. She's always there; just behind you, just out of view. But never out of earshot. She tells you the truth: that you're annoying, You're a burden. You're always just there. You're never enough. You're a disappointment. You're a liability. It's all your fault. Everyone hates you. You're worthless. You're stupid. You're clueless. You're such a fuck up.

You don't know what it's like to feel too scared to reach out for help. Too scared to message your friend for fear or being rejected. Abandoned. Of being too scared to reach out because you'll upset them. Because you don't know why they put up with you in the first place. You don't know what it's like to genuinely believe that no-one likes you. To

genuinely believe that they're going to walk
away and leave you, any day now. Any minute.

You don't know what it's like to be so desperate
to speak to someone that you send the message
anyway, despite that fear.
Because you just need someone to talk to.
You're sure they won't reply. You're too intense.
They haven't got time for your shit.

But wait. They replied. They're fine. They're
lovely.

Relief.

See. I told you you were stupid for thinking that
they hate you.

But now you scrutinise their message, looking
for any indication that you're annoying them.
That you're too much of a burden and they want
you to leave them alone – but they're too polite
to tell you.

Hate. I hate myself. I hate that I'm like this.

You don't know what it's like to make that tiny
pin prick. To see the little drop of blood and feel
the relief surge out of you. Instant.

You don't know what it's like to watch that pin prick turn into a slice from a blade, the tiny drop turns into a trickle, which turns into a flood.
You don't know what it's like to crave that. To need it. You usually do it to let out the anxiety. To ground you. To remind you you're still alive. The sting as you make that slice reminds you you're real.
The pain that takes away just a little bit of the pain inside. Sometimes though, you do it just to hurt yourself. You do it because you deserve it. You don't know what it's like to feel the frustration when it doesn't work like it normally does. So you go deeper.

You don't know what it's like to want the scars. To obsess over wanting those scars on your arm because even though you hide them, they scream out: "I'm not okay."
They're proof. Proof that you feel this way. Proof that it isn't all in your head.

You don't know what it's like to ache inside. To cry so hard you physically hurt. To genuinely believe everyone would be better if you weren't around. You don't know what it's like to have sat, at 4am, broken. Sobbing while calculating the amount of paracetamol it will take. Not enough to require a hospital admission, but

enough to make them see you. You don't want to
die, you want to self harm. This is a good way.
A new way. But you didn't take them. Not this
time.

You don't know what it's like to feel so scared.
To know you're losing everything, everyone you
care about. You're so annoying and they're
getting sick of you, and by doing this you're
pushing them away. You know you are, so you
stop. You hide.
But then you feel a surge of unknown emotion.
It scares you, so you cling. You send them a
message, to put your mind at ease. But then you
realise you shouldn't have done that. The
shadow reminds you that they're having a lovely
time doing whatever they're doing, but now
they're reminded of you. You've ruined their
day now, you selfish bitch. So you send another
message, an apology. Now you're bombarding
them. For fuck's sake.

Why am I like this?

Do you really think they give that much of a
shit? You really think one message from you
impacts their day? So self centred. So vain.
You're nothing special babe, get over yourself.

You don't know what it's like to think and think
and think and think. About everything. You can't
keep track, there's so much and it's all too fast.
You replay every conversation a hundred
thousand times, over and over, scrutinising every
millisecond; every word; every slight change in
their body language. Finding the things that you
did or said wrong. So repetitive, and yet you
don't understand a word.

You don't know what it's like to have a war
inside your head. There's a voice in there,
screaming at someone. Someone screams back.
You can't always make out what they're saying,
but they're yelling. They're yelling at you.
You can't silence it. You can't block it out. You
can't stop it. You can't think of anything else. It
just won't. go. away. You don't know how
exhausting it is fighting that battle every single
day.

You don't know what it's like to be unable to sit
still. So restless. To pace, back and forth. To
have to really focus, just to breathe. You're
worried about something. The shadow is telling
you something awful is going to happen - you
can feel it, but you don't know what it is.
Just breathe. In and out. Your back is prickling.
Your arms and hands are tingling. You're getting

lightheaded. You can't breathe. Sit down. No,
you have to move. Pace. You're sweating. It's so
hot. You're not breathing properly. Why can't
you breathe properly? What's happening?
You're SO hot! Get onto the floor, you're going
to faint. You're dizzy. Everything is spinning.
Just stay still. Knees against your chest. I can't
breathe. I can't breathe.

Just breathe.

In and out.

In and out.

In and out.

Five things you can see.
Four things you can feel.
Three things you can hear.
Two things you can smell.
One thing you can taste.
It's passing. It's passing.

It's colder now. You're covered in sweat, but
you're shivering.

For one blissful moment, the shadow has shut
up.

But then, she's back. She's screaming again.
You're writhing around, crying, trying to get
away, but she's there, reminding you that
everyone hates you. You're annoying. They'd be
better if you were dead.

This is pointless. What's the point in any of it?
Did you know some ants can live for 25 years?
25 years. Of carrying things around. What a life.
What's the point in that?

How good would it be to just go to sleep, and
never wake up? Bliss.

You don't know what it's like to be so totally
exhausted that you can barely get out of bed. To
have no energy whatsoever. But your friend the
shadow is there to remind you that those calories
won't burn themselves.

You don't know what it's like to look in the
mirror and hate what you see. You might know
what it's like to be unhappy with the way that
you look. To find aspects you'd like to change,
but you don't know what it's like to grab
handfuls of fat on your stomach, and thighs. To
cry as you try desperately to wrench them from
your body. You don't know what it's like to

flinch away from any reflective surface because
the sight of yourself is loathsome. That shadow
is still there.

You make me sick.

You don't know what it's like to starve yourself.
To feel that agonising growl in your stomach,
but to love it. To know that it's working. You'll
lose weight. You've missed your period. It's
working! You feel dizzy when you stand up –
it's working. Your hip bones are starting to stick
out – it's working!!!
You can do this. You can do anything! You're
smashing it! You're winning! You feel amazing,
like superwoman. You can run further than you
ever have before. You don't even really get
hungry now! Water works just as well.

But you can hear the whispers. Your friends are
talking about you. They're all talking about you.
They don't believe you're trying. They hate you
and they just want you out. They can't see it
how you do. They can't understand. And
equally, you don't understand them. So you turn
to the shadow. You confide in her, you listen to
her. She's all you need. She understands.

You don't know what it's like to crave doughnuts so badly that you sit on the bathroom floor and eat a pack of five, fully intending to throw them straight back up again. You're desperately trying to make sure it all comes back out, wailing as you retch until nothing comes up but bile. Only then can you be sure they're gone. That no calories remain. You're disgusted at yourself. You didn't even enjoy the doughnuts.

You don't know what it's like to stare at a biscuit for half an hour. To choose not to eat it and feel so proud of yourself for resisting. You're miserable, because you can't think of anything else. All you want is that damn biscuit.
But you're doing it; you're losing weight! So it's worth it.

You don't know what it's like to cry over a slice of toast. The unbearable guilt when you actually enjoy eating it. You don't know what it's like to have a full on panic attack, all because of one fucking milkshake. You know you have to eat, because otherwise you'll be admitted to hospital. But every time you do, that shadow reminds you you're such a fat cow. That you don't deserve it. You need to carry on restricting – shrink. Shrink. Shrink.

You don't know what it's like to have to force
yourself to eat, even though everything inside
you is screaming that you shouldn't do it. It goes
against every instinct you have. The conflict is
unbearable. You're arguing with yourself.
Always. If you do eat, they'll think you're okay.
They'll think it's easy, because you've done it.
They think it's all about weight. But they don't
know how much you're hurting.

You're trying so, so hard, but it's not working.
Everything you do falls apart, despite your
efforts. This is too hard.

You don't know what it's like to know, logically,
that what you're doing makes absolutely no
sense. You know that. But you don't believe it.
The shadow doesn't believe it. She's always
there to remind you – those extra ten calories
will make you obese. You'll be fat again
tomorrow. The rules don't apply to you, not like
they do to everyone else. One slice of cake
won't make them fat. But you can't eat it. If you
do, you'll never stop. Greedy. You'll lose all
control.

You don't know what it's like to deal with all
this shit. Day in, and day out. There's no respite.
You don't get a day off. It's relentless.

You don't know what it's like to live with these mental illnesses.

And do you know what? I hope you never, ever have to find out.

Testing the Alternatives

The ice works. It's that good kind of pain,
without leaving a scar.

But I want the scars. So badly.
Why? Why do I want fucking scars?

I want them to tell the story of this part of my
life.
Like validation maybe?
I don't know.

There is so much of this shit I don't know.

Me and My ED

I really don't understand this eating disorder.
I'm terrified of gaining weight, I'm terrified of
eating too much.

I don't let myself eat. I'm so, so hungry.
All I want to do is eat, but I just can't let myself.

I talk to people about it, and they don't
understand it.
Rightly so; I don't understand it either.

I want to get help. I am getting help.
But I know it's going to be really hard,
and I don't know how I'm going to do it.

It Gets Easier

There are days when it's lighter
Days when you can smile
There are days when you feel better
Yeah, it's been a while.

Life isn't always going to be hard
Hold on to the reprieve
I revel in this feeling
And pray it doesn't leave.

One thing that I know for sure
Is that happiness doesn't last
I'm waiting for the ball to drop
For when present becomes past.

Because before I know it
Here comes the inner pain
Lost and tired and hopeless,
When my world goes dark again.

Splitting

I'm so scared of losing you.
You're all I can think about.
When I see you my heart sings.
When we say goodbye it breaks.
I love you; don't leave me.

You're the best thing in my life
And I'm not whole when you're not around.
I don't tell you this because I'm scared
you'll leave me if I do.

You'll tell me if I'm too much, won't you?
You assure me that you will
You tell me it's okay
and my heart sings again.
I love you; don't leave me.

Why haven't you replied?
Or told me you love me back?
I'm too much for you aren't i?
I'll give you a break - you deserve a break.

And then I see you.
And I'm so scared I've upset you.
I tell you and you say everything is fine.

You're the best friend I could ask for; I don't
deserve you.
I love you; don't leave me.

But then you don't reply.
I'm sorry. I'm terrified that you'll leave me.
You act as though everything is fine.
It isn't fine. I'm not fine.
Why can't you see it?

I hate you.
You're the one person I thought I could trust.
You're the one who said all along that I could
talk to you any time, and that you were always
there. Turns out you're a liar.
Because you haven't replied.
I hate you; don't leave me.

When It Doesn't Work

I'd made up my mind earlier in the day.
Became certain that it was my last.
That wasn't the first time i'd try this;
There had been many more in the past.

This time was so different though;
It was hope that made me sure
I prayed for it all to be over now,
As I sat motionless on the floor.

I'd written the note, left it out to be found
and I cried and I cried and I cried
at the thought of saying goodbye to you all
but life is too hard; I've tried.

I picked up the blade and I made the first cut
as deep as I could go.
I expected it to be instant; my life would be done
Instead, just a gentle red flow.

It didn't hurt; angrily I did it again,
Two more, three more, four.
But I didn't die; and my heart sank down
As I lay there alone on the floor.

Looking back now, I don't understand
why I really thought that would work.
The surge of disappointment will always remain
The sadness inside me still lurks.

So I picked myself up and reached out for
support,
Turns out this wasn't my time.
I got the wounds cleaned, they increased my
meds
and I told everybody: 'I'm fine'.

Though that wasn't the last time I would try this
again
There have been so many more attempts since
I don't understand why i'm so bad at this
I wake up the next day, and wince.

This life I must continue to live
In truth, things aren't still that dark
I can see brighter days now, it's not quite that
bad
I'm slowly regaining my spark.

The Monster In My Head

When I was younger I was scared
Of the monsters under my bed
Now I'm grown all I'm scared of
Is the monster in my head

Being with you, talking to you
That monster felt so small
But when you weren't around me
It grew, became my all.

The way that it all ended
And all the things you said
Made it clear that I'd become
The monster in my head.

For all I say about you
And all the hate I feel
There's so much more for myself
Me, the monster made real.

I never wanted to make you
Feel I was the toxic friend
But now I see that's all I am
When will this hatred end?

I tried so hard to stop it
I tried my best to be
The person that you wanted
That you deserved; not me.

That's all in the past now
I'm desperate to move on
But the fear still haunts me
Of the monster I've become.

Hypomania

Delusions of grandeur
The God complex
I feel invincible at times
Like I can conquer the world

I start so many projects
And I know I can smash them all
I feel on top of the world
The best I've ever been

I can paint the next great art piece
Write a novel, a sitcom, a book of poems
Learn the piano or violin
I buy them all in full faith that I can do it

Life is amazing; I've never been so happy
I don't even need to sleep - a few hours a night
is enough
And then the doubt creeps in
Try as I might to block it out

I come to a halt; the thoughts get dark
I realise I can't do it at all
I try and cling on but things fall through the
cracks

I can't do anything any more

I search for inspiration, watch Fleabag, read
poems
It makes me understand I'll never be Phoebe
Waller Bridge
Or come even close to her level of genius
Why did I even try?

Fears For The Future

I don't know what I'm more scared of;
the thought that it will work
of the thought that it won't.

Who Am I?

I used to think I knew myself.
My life was on track and I was sure
I knew what I wanted, what I liked, who I loved
But then you came along and made me question
everything.

I loved the glow you emitted
the joy you brought into every room.
You were such a great person and I fell in head
over heels
You know exactly who you are and you really
work to achieve it.

I loved that about you the most
You're unlike anyone else I've ever known.
And as my adoration for you grew, it took away
my feelings that I even know what I want any
more.

There's something about being around perfect
people
it brings out my own imperfections.
More and more I was inspired by you, but
it made me more focused on the me I don't
know.

These feelings of emptiness grow and grow
Some days it's all I can find inside me
that hollowness is there all the time now
I've lost myself. The me I once knew is long
gone.

I don't know who I am any more
I don't know what I want.
I just want to feel whole again;
but that feeling is long gone.

We Must Talk

Before I experienced my own mental illness
I thought I understood it quite well
I didn't know about it growing up
But one lecture at Uni and caring for people
with common mental illnesses made me think
that I had it figured out.

But then it hit me and sent me reeling;
Depression isn't just being sad.
Anxiety isn't occasional panic attacks.
Anorexia isn't just being scared of food.
Addiction is just not being able to stop.
I'd never even heard of borderline personality
disorder.

Mental illness is talked about much more now
But I feel like it still isn't enough.
Children need to be educated about it
Stigmatising words and thoughts need to be
eradicated
Health professionals need support and more than
1 lecture.

And for people themselves who are living with
this

We need, and deserve better.
I shouldn't have to fight for the care that I need.
I shouldn't have to educate others on how to
speak to me
I shouldn't have had to attempt to end my life
to finally get through to someone about my
medication.

Yes, things are getting better. Society is learning
to talk
But what about the stigma that still surrounds?
The whispers? The fear? The hiding and
pretending?
The lack of fucking funding? Why is this still
happening?

We. Must. Talk.

Impulsive

Impulsive

Adjective: A fleeting thought leads to instant action, that you undoubtedly later regret but can't seem to stop yourself from repeating over and over and fucking over again.

See also:
Self harm
Reckless spending
Continually changing small things that you can
Promiscuity and unsafe sex
Agreeing to things on the spur of the moment (that you're definitely going to have to find a way out of)

Dissociation

I walked along the pavement
And slowly realised
that I had no idea how i'd got there
I feel as though someone else is in control.

I sit alone in the bath tub
and suddenly recall
that the water is cold; but it wasn't before.
I feel as though someone else is in control.

I'm lying on my bed
with a podcast playing in the background
I tune back in and have no idea what they're
talking about.
I feel as though someone else is in control.

I come back to my own body
It's sitting on the floor, there's a blade, there's
blood.
There's pain, but I can't remember doing that.
I feel as though someone else is in control.

There are times when I feel ethereal
I could be a ghost, I'm translucent.
The choices I make aren't mine; I don't know.

I feel as though someone else is in control.

The Person I've Become

I've tried so hard to get used to
the extreme emotional states.
How quickly my moods fluctuate
and the searing pain they make me feel.

I really fucking hate
this person I've become.

I've really worked on my impulsivity
I try to think things through.
Though of course I still act on thoughts alone
And regret almost everything as soon as it's
done.

I really fucking hate
this person I've become.

I've taught myself to eat again,
despite the voice in my head.
I've gained so much weight and i'm trying to
accept it
But i'm desperate to fall back into that trap.

I really fucking hate
this person I've become.

I've lost so many friendships
Became a monster, a truly toxic friend.
The paranoia made me untrusting and awful
But those friends I do have left are really
amazing ones.

I really fucking hate
this person I've become.

Yes, my medications have changed me
but i'm better than before.
I'm not suicidal all the time, I don't cry
endlessly.
I've lost the me I used to be, but maybe it's not
all that bad?

I think I've come to terms with
The person I've become.